A Rowing Boat
to Freedom

Douglas Maas

ISBN: 979-8-8051-1762-7

To

I dedicate this account to my own lovely family and their successors. It will be seen that, in places, I appear to be speaking to them directly because that was the original purpose. This began life as a simple document to let them know something of their origins, should they have an interest and wish to know. I hope this revised and expanded version will add even more to their understanding of some of what came before.

In the process, as the account reveals, I became ever more acutely aware of the need to pass on the wider story to any greater interested audience. I hope everyone understands its mission and finds it of interest.

In memory

When my parents were alive, I was not old enough to have been interested enough in their history, to my regret. Sadly we knew each other for only a handful of years.

In Memory of my Dad: I like to think of this as some kind of lasting memory of my Dad whose life before I knew him was certainly remarkable, dramatic and so sad, though I knew very little of all that during the time I knew him.
The events which affected him and his family (and me) must not be forgotten.

It is also of course **in memory of my lovely Mum** who had a much more 'ordinary' life (until she married my Dad!). I remember her with great affection. In particular I am sad that I knew her for an even shorter time.

CONTENTS

ACKNOWLEDGEMENTS

I merely and humbly acknowledge the sources of all the numerous pieces of information, photographs, etc. which I have acquired over my lifetime. Some are specific and I acknowledge those writings by including them in the References section, at the end.

Mostly, I am grateful to those sources of numerous tiny pieces of the jigsaw which have gradually seeped into my understanding during the past 70 years or so.

PHOTOGRAPHS

There are a few photographs here. Mostly they are not mine and I have no idea who pressed the button on whose camera. It was a long time ago.

1 INTRODUCTION

The train slowed down, approaching the station. Ernst Cohn had been watching the gathering darkness outside. The 800 kilometre journey from Berlin had seemed never-ending. He had changed trains twice, showing papers and ticket. Heart stopping moments. It had been an uncomfortable journey, quite apart from his own terrible misgivings about the momentous decision he had made. It was 1935. Uniforms were everywhere. The slow steam trains had made many clanking stops on the journey south. Ernst had endured it silently, remaining seated and as inconspicuous as possible. He was wearing a faded raincoat over a grey business suit. His homburg-style hat had been on the seat next to him. Now, he put it on his head. His slim attaché case was his only luggage.

These were terrible, worrying times. Less than 24 hours ago and in an instant, Ernst's life had been completely changed when he had received that devastating message in the firm's Berlin office. He had needed to make some enormous decisions very quickly; decisions which would utterly affect the rest of his life in ways he couldn't possibly imagine. Indeed, getting it right or wrong now could mean life or death, one way or another. He would not get another chance. Ernst was 37 years old.

He had made his irretrievable decision. It would be a journey into the unknown but it was really the only option. With little delay he had hurried from the office and walked as quickly as he dare to Berlin's railway station - the Bahnhof. There had been just enough Reichsmarks in his wallet to buy a single ticket. Now he fingered that ticket, checking it was still in his waistcoat pocket. He nervously looked around.

The squeal of wheels on the curve and a clatter over the points signalled arrival. The train lurched to a stop. Trying not to appear hurried, he got off and walked steadily along the platform. At the barrier he handed the ticket to the official, then slipped away into the unfamiliar shadows. The next few hours would seal his fate.

Ernst had a sketchy idea of how he might escape. He would need a great deal of luck. There were gas lights. It took time to walk inconspicuously through the dim streets. In a while he sensed the presence of the river which he knew would be there. But how could he cross that big river? Any bridges would be guarded. Somehow, he must cross to the far side. His life would almost certainly depend on it. Impossible now to turn back.

In the pale dim moonlight, leaving the streets behind, he found a way to the river bank and carefully walked along it. After a while a small boathouse loomed in the darkness. It was open to the river and inside he could just see what he was hoping for. The luck he needed - a rowing boat lay alongside the narrow jetty. A pair of oars lay loosely inside.

As much by feel as by sight, Ernst untied the boat and stepped into it. As quietly as possible, he sorted out the oars and pushed off, beginning the long pull across the wide, flowing river. His mind was racing. Could his journey have been discovered? Was there a search for him, even now closing in. Was this really the best plan? It was far too late now for doubts or for turning back.

Surely the boat would be noticed in the moonlight? Even in the gloom he was a sitting target. He expected there would be a shout, then another and then machine gun fire. Second only to those nerve-jangling thoughts came an overwhelming sense of despair. He wondered about the chances of ever seeing his wife Ursel and his daughter Irene again. Would he survive? Would they survive? Would he ever see his home town again, his country again, his elderly mother Henriette, his brothers and sisters, his friends? His oldest brother Fritz had already been taken. How would his other siblings fare? He - Ernst - was leaving them all behind and could never return.

There were no shouts, no gunfire. Despite the turmoil in his head, all around was calm. After what seemed an endless time, pulling the oars hard against the strong current, being carried downstream, the boat neared the opposite bank. The bows grounded on the shore. Being careful and precise, befitting his profession, Ernst pulled the boat up onto the bank as far as he could so that it wouldn't drift, with the slight but vain hope that the owner would be able to retrieve it. He shipped the oars neatly, stood up and looked briefly around. Moving away from the river into the moonlit darkness, he paused for a moment to consider his bearings.

He had escaped! Ernst had crossed the mighty River Rhine

undetected and had arrived safely in Switzerland. His conflicting emotions were tumbling through his head but he knew he must stay focussed. The task which lay ahead was momentous. Could he accomplish it and survive? There was no longer any decision to be made. There was only one direction to take. He firmly gripped his attaché case and began to walk.

Perhaps, reading that, you believed you had picked up a novel or short story in error. No, the core of that account is as factual as I can discover. I have imagined some of the details. Maybe over-imagined, maybe not. They are included to broadly illustrate something of what must have happened. Precisely how Ernst travelled south from Berlin that day (or days) is unknown. He must have made that journey somehow. I am sure it bears no resemblance to how it would be done today.

Ernst was my father and the essentials of that story - my hearing about that crossing of a river in a rowing boat in the darkness - is amongst the earliest clear recollections of my life. That image has stayed with me constantly. As a young son, it led me to think that my father should write a book of his adventures. This particular adventure was clearly just a tiny part of his story which gradually, during the rest of my life, has unfolded to me. What follows here is my own attempt to try to correct that omission of a book for him.

But my father never talked about his adventures (if that is what they should be called). Piece by piece since then, during my 77 years, I have assembled a lot of the jigsaw, though there will always be many missing pieces. Some years ago I began to keep notes so that my family would have some knowledge of all this, as well as some of my own somewhat varied history. Those notes form the basis of my autobiography - The (Un)eventful Life of Douglas E. Maas (75 years from WW-2 to Covid-19), which has so far only been seen by my family. This small book is essentially just the first chapter of that story. I thought it deserved its own life, for the reasons I explain in the following pages.

A few anecdotes are remembered from childhood experience and curiosity. Subsequently many more have been gleaned from discussions with my dear, late sister Irene (Reni) who was really my half-sister, 18 years older than me. The book written by my cousin Gabriella Mautner, The Good Place, has also been a valuable source of background information. My cousin Franz who I have never met has written a compelling account to which I will refer. My mother's sister-in-law - my late Auntie Edna - as well as cousin John, have also provided a few snippets and some photographs about my mother and about my young life, which is very briefly referred to here. My son, Glenn, has done some research too.

As I gradually compiled my notes over the years it became clear that my father's story deserved separate treatment. It was also in my mind that my grandchildren and their descendants - well into the future - might want to know something of the origins of our name 'Maas' because there is a frequent need to try to explain this to others and always the temptation to dismiss it by replying, "Oh, it's a long story!". In 2018 this part of the story therefore became a separate short document, which has now been revived, updated and expanded here.

Of course, the following pages tell the story of the river crossing plus some of the events which led up to it and what happened next.

Now, in my later years, I feel my heritage quite deeply. All of this is the reason I am here.

The following account is the substance of what I know about my Dad's history. I hope it also conveys a tiny part of the much larger story which really must be told. Those words tend to get repeated and I do not apologise. I am acutely conscious that, at the time of preparing this for publication - March/April 2022, the world is nervous of some kind of repetition.

Douglas Edward Maas
Charnwood Forest
April 2022

"How can it be that any human being can hate another - or even an entire race - so much?"

2   WHY ARE WE CALLED MAAS?

(the important story to know - by reading this brief account - and to pass on so that nobody forgets)

above: Me, my Mum Helen, my half-sister Irene (Reni) and my Dad, Ernst. Probably Victoria Park, Leicester c1948

Since their beginning, human beings have only developed their understanding and progressed by telling stories. I have discovered that telling some stories can be vitally important. I believe that this is one such story. We must not overlook it. Additionally, my family and others of coming generations could find it especially interesting. I am writing this primarily for them but it is a tiny part of a massive subject of interest to many.

Some might wonder why our family name is 'Maas'. They will get asked that from time to time. They will certainly be the need to spell the name on numerous occasions and will have to correct many misspellings. Even pronunciation can be a challenge (it should be like a refined 'glass' or 'grass' rather than vase or mass). It isn't easy to give a simple explanation of its origin and it is easy to avoid the subject by saying, "Oh, it's a long story" but sometimes it can be helpful to give an explanation.

This small book contains that explanation. Please read and take an interest. Please note the wider story and pass it on. To the family (future generations, whether or not their name is Maas, are sure to want to know) and to anyone else. Please don't just dismiss it by saying, "Oh, it's a long story".

... and for that matter, why is my name 'Douglas'?

This account isn't about me (other than my family name) - it's primarily about my Dad and his family. I have written elsewhere about my life - the continuing story - at some length with a lot more detail! If my family is interested enough to want to know more about me, they can discover it all.

But here, first, I have to explain how this short and specific account of my Dad and his family came to be written.

I was born in Leicester, England on 17th May 1944. There was still a year to go before the end of the War. Rationing. Bomb craters. National dried milk and orange juice for children. Coal fires, smoking chimneys and smog. Exciting tram rides into town. Recycle all brown wrapping paper, string, absolutely everything. Newspaper for toilet paper and to make Christmas decorations. A grey world. Just the wireless - no TV. My Mum Helen was a Leicester working girl and an active Christian church-goer. She was my Dad's second wife and she met him (probably in 1938, I'm guessing) while she was working at the machines in a Leicester knitwear factory. She married the boss!

For much of my early life, my Dad's origins and family have been a rather vague mystery. Kids generally don't want to know. They grow up and then involve themselves in their own family's busy lives and only later in life do they start compiling family trees and sometimes take more of an interest in their ancestry. From my own early-years perspective it was very plain that - although my Dad was wonderful, albeit a bit 'different' - his relatives were very different. Clearly rather 'foreign'. My dear (half) sister Reni has attributed it to 'different cultures'. Yes, I agree - it all seemed so different at my young age. So sadly, at that time, I kept other members of his family at arms-length. These days I am sorry for having done so and for my lack of understanding all those years ago.

Throughout my life I have gradually acquired, bit by bit, an understanding of what this story was all about - it is only in quite recent years that I have taken a pro-active interest. Reni (18 years older than me) has answered many questions and she remembered quite a lot. Sadly I can no longer ask her as my dear sister died in December 2017. Some time ago I bought a copy of my cousin Gaby's book, The Good Place and have also obtained a copy of my cousin Franz's own account, We Live On. We have met up with my second cousin Barbara and her husband James in London. That was a pleasure. Long ago, as a child or teenager, I did meet five of Dad's brothers and sisters, two of them quite regularly. Of course, they and many of their children are gone now (I am inevitably a generation younger than most of my first cousins). I was never to meet two of Dad's siblings, my Uncle Fritz and my Aunt Marianne. But they are an important part of this account.

I deeply regret that Dad didn't tell me more of his early life. It was seldom mentioned and at a young and busy age I had no reason to ask. I was 24 when he died. This account hopes to avoid that happening in the case of my family.

... "Why is our name Maas?"

As part of that taking an interest, in 2018 I made a valuable and, to me, very significant visit to the National Holocaust Centre and Museum at Laxton, near Newark - www.holocaust.org.uk - not so far away. You don't go there for a "fun day out" but to understand, to reflect, to remember (and even be deeply moved and saddened). You vow to pass on what happened, in the hope that it can never happen again. While there I joined in with a large group of Year 5 children and other visitors to listen to a 'Survivor', 90-year old Hedi Argent, who told her story and how she came to England.

Hedi emphasised, more than anything, why she was telling her story. So that everyone knows ... and doesn't forget. Of course I have been well aware but this experience made me doubly convinced about the importance of telling this story - it is a large part of the reason for this small book.

The story is an integral part of our family's story. I wish I had known more and really wish I had taken more interest at an earlier age and had been able to pass on the story much earlier. But Dad never talked about it.

For my family, the events of those years are an inescapable part of our history - why we are here at all - and why our name is Maas.

My Father was born 14th January 1898 - his name was Ernst Heinrich Cohn

So, there you have it - the reason for this account. Why isn't our name Cohn? "Why is our name Maas?"

Dad was born in Chemnitz. This place is now, and was then, an industrial German city in Saxony near to the Czech border. When Germany was partitioned after World War 2, this became part of East Germany and the city was re-named KarlMarxStadt during the partition years but regained its original name upon re-unification.

My Dad was the second youngest of eight brothers and sisters born into a Jewish business family there (significantly, Dad's mother's maiden name was Maas). The family tree - not compiled by me - needs some study but can be worked out, given time and an interest in doing so. It partly takes us back to 1722 and to my Great Great Great Grandfather, Samuel Götz Kohn (1722-1792) in Schwerin, northern Germany. His wife was Rachel Kohn (nee Joel) (1747-1811).

Dad on holiday at Pragelato in the mountains near Turin, Italy August 1933 - the year it all began ...

I have very little direct information about my Dad's childhood and young life. He loved the Black Forest and spent holidays there, including a bit of Winter cross-country ski-ing. Other than

9

that, he was not a sportsman - and so nor am I! But I learned a good deal from my cousin Gaby's book (*The Good Place*, Gabriella Mautner) which describes a similar, parallel existence because Gaby and Reni were a similar age and lived in similar circumstances. Gabriella (Gaby) is the daughter of Dad's sister Lotte and her husband Norbert Kramer who owned a substantial business in the hosiery trade (significant). To Gaby they are Mutti and Vati and referred to as such in her book. Reading the book gives me many echoes of that history to compare with my own childhood memories. Names of their friends, family and associates crop up as being familiar to me - Schwab, Bonwitt, Sigler - and some of the brothers' and sisters' activities and pastimes clearly transferred as their interests in their later lives. It also gives some information about what life was like in Germany in the years leading up to World War 2.

On a visit to Reni in the USA in 2013 I acquired some copies of photographs of Dad and his family. Until then I had never seen such early pictures and so they are very special to me. A few are reproduced here and some are included in the collages which have been framed and hang on our wall and those of our grown up children.

When the First World War broke out in 1914, Dad would have been 16 years old. I first realised the implications of this a long time ago and it made me feel uncomfortable. Yes, my Dad served in the German Army during that War. Reni has confirmed it. But of course it was simply a fact of life that young men served their own country that way. I am sure they had to. I am convinced that Dad has always been a peace-loving guy and his army service would have been done reluctantly. He survived.

Following the end of that War in 1918, it was clear that the terrible conflict and tremendous loss of life had solved nothing. Crucially, for my Dad and his family (and countless millions of others), the seeds had been sown for what was to come.

Dad attended two universities (I seem to remember being told they were at Heidelberg and Freiburg, though I might be wrong). He obtained his PhD in Organic Chemistry at Karlsruhe in 1924. (I wonder if it could be googled!). His research was into discovering a method of bleaching wool to enable the subsequent coloured dyes to be more vibrant and therefore the product better quality. This expertise led him to become involved with his brother-in-law Norbert's hosiery business which (as Gaby's book tells us) was a global business. This fact is significant as the story develops.

He was impacted by the hyper-inflation period in Weimar Germany. Money sent to him at University was worthless by the time it reached him! Very difficult times. (What, no student loans?). He returned from university to Chemnitz and about 1924/25 (I assume the date) married Ursel Ulrich. Their daughter, Irene Cohn (ultimately to be my half-sister) was born on 27th July 1926. To me and some others, she has always been known as Reni.

I am totally unqualified to write about the plight of Jewish people and so, at this point, I will cover this massive but essential subject in a short paragraph. Millions of Jewish people had lived their lives throughout Europe ever since Roman times. Their history goes back much further. They were in every respect just ordinary folk, rich and poor, farm labourers and business people, going about their daily lives. But they were a "minority" which was hated by some and, from time to time during the past two millennia, they have been persecuted. Antisemitism appears to be still rife. It is a fundamental part of the history of the World that different peoples hate one another. I certainly will not attempt to explain it here because I just do not understand how this happens. How can it be that any human being can hate another - or even an entire race - so much? Often, it seems, for religious reasons. I simply cannot comprehend it, but it has happened throughout history and is happening now, around the world. Even in the UK, it seems there are people who want it to happen again, right now. It is a fact of history and is thus well documented. A massive subject. You will have to study that for yourself. The story of the Jews in particular is extremely well told at the Holocaust Centre.

And now - here is another big subject. At about the same time that Dad was at university and then married - the 1920s - something was happening which was to affect the lives of everyone - even us and our name! That time saw the beginnings of the rise of an Austrian-born man called Adolf Hitler who came to Germany and developed his theories about what should comprise a perfect Germany. Again, it is a vast subject which anyone interested should look into themselves. Hitler wrote his manifesto for how this should be achieved - Mein Kampf - while serving a five year prison term.

But the relevant point was that Adolf Hitler hated Jews, together with other minorities such as gipsies, disabled people and homosexuals. He wanted Germany to comprise a 'pure race' of blonde, fit, blue-eyed Aryan people, taking the science of eugenics to the extreme. History has of course described him as a 'mad-man'. Because of the great uncertainties following their defeat in the First World War, the economic uncertainties, even the Wall Street crash, the people of Germany were in a parlous state and were searching for new hope. By a series of well-documented political moves, the creation of the Nazi Party and as a powerful personality and orator, Adolf Hitler steadily rose through the political system to become the German Chancellor. Ultimately he had no challenger. He seemed to offer the German people the hope they were desperate for. By 1933 most of them were blindly following him. It all happened very quickly. For many years, there would be no turning back.

Hitler's goal was to be achieved by creating an expanding super-race of Germans who would enlarge the country by conquering others to acquire more space for economic development and, crucially, to simply eliminate everyone who failed that test of being a fit blonde-haired, blue-eyed German.

That meant - eliminate gipsies, eliminate disabled people, eliminate the Jews.

It is such a big, mind-boggling subject. I won't even attempt it here. There are numerous sources of information to study and to try to understand it all.

In practice, initially, this meant that no Jews were allowed to simply continue their lives as they had always done. They could not simply hold onto and continue with their jobs, as teachers, doctors, lawyers, professionals as before. Their premises were confiscated. They were evicted from their homes. They could only get medical treatment from Jewish doctors who practised in rooms in the houses which remained. They could only buy food in the few remaining Jewish shops. Children led miserable lives at school as they were shunned and seriously bullied by other children who were egged-on by their indoctrinated parents. School teachers were forced to teach the Nazi doctrine. Jewish teachers held classes at their own homes, under very difficult circumstances. It all happened very quickly.

Late at night, there would be a knock on the door and men were brought out of the house in their dressing gowns and made to scrub the pavement with their toothbrush. Total humiliation. Many men disappeared - taken to concentration camps, possibly to be seen again as broken men. Thousands were never seen again.

Jewish premises were labelled with a big painted star of David. Non-Jews were told never to shop there. Jews were made to wear big yellow badges identifying themselves as such. Bit by bit the situation became much worse and ever more serious and difficult for the Jewish families.

Later, there was Kristallnacht (the night of crystal/glass) on November 9 to November 10, 1938. In two days and nights, more than 1,000 synagogues were burned to the ground or seriously damaged. Rioters ransacked and looted about 7,500 Jewish businesses, killed at least 91 Jews, and vandalized Jewish hospitals, homes, schools, and cemeteries. The attackers were often neighbours. Some 30,000 Jewish males aged 16 to 60 were arrested. To accommodate so many new prisoners, the concentration camps at Dachau, Buchenwald, and Sachsenhausen were expanded. (NB: Simon Parkin's book, 'The Island of Extraordinary Captives' gives a chilling explanation of what led up to Kristallnacht).

Prior to Kristallnacht, the Nazi policies described had been primarily non-violent. But Kristallnacht was to be the turning point and conditions for German Jews then grew increasingly much worse. Violence against the Jews increased.

Even non-Jewish Germans didn't escape - their disabled people including their disabled children were taken away to institutions and 'exterminated'. Yes, the story of that period is a chilling one but worse, much worse, was to come.

During World War 2 (1939-45), Hitler and the Nazis implemented their so-called 'Final Solution' to deal with what they referred to as the 'Jewish problem' and carried out the systematic murder of some 6 million European Jews in what came to be known as the Holocaust. In total, 11 million people were murdered this way. Altogether, 26 million (or more) people died in World War 2 - all as a result of the 'madness' of Adolf Hitler.

Is this enough reason for this story to be told, as often as possible, in the hope that such madness can never be repeated?

OK, we're getting ahead of ourselves. Let's look back a bit and see what was happening to my Dad and his family. If you'd like more background please read my cousin Gaby's book The Good Place. It describes what happened to her family during these years and it must therefore be very similar to what happened to our family. Another very good and 'real' account is given in the novel by Ben Elton - Two Brothers. My family should find a couple of copies around. And there is endless literature and film of the subject.

In the early 1930's it would have been difficult to foresee the ultimate events. But it was clear to Jews that things were not looking good. Why didn't they leave before it was too late?

The explanation is that, for the majority, this really would have been an enormous ask!

Firstly you needed a very good reason to want to leave your home country (and your friends, relatives, work, institutions) which you have loved all your life. Your own country which you have probably served well and which, until now, has served you well. Anyone needs a very good and considered reason to emigrate. Secondly they needed the wherewithal to buy the tickets, if nothing else. Money and property had been confiscated. Thirdly they need somewhere to go! Countries always have resisted - and no doubt always will resist - taking in refugees. Especially those who are bringing no money, don't even speak the language and will probably need looking after in some way. Humanitarian good intent can only stretch so far. Too much of a burden on space, resources, the system, everything. So, while departure from Germany was initially not forbidden by the Nazis it was in fact almost impossible to do, for most.

Having said that, 300,000 Jews (a relatively small number) did leave Germany between 1933 and 1939. My Dad and most of his brothers and sisters were among them. It wasn't easy. Incidentally, at about the same time - 1934 - and in a similar way, Anne Frank (her Diary) and her family left for The Netherlands, as did my Dad and his daughter Reni who was a similar age, as described later. It might almost have been a parallel story.

There also developed a system whereby children could be transported out to other sympathetic countries. It became known as Kindertransport. It depended on very generous and selfless people in those countries being willing to help and actively organise the arrangements and, especially, provide a home for the children. 10,000 came this way to the UK and smaller numbers to a few other countries. A tiny but important number. The only possessions the children could have with them must be contained in one very small suitcase. No money.

They had to leave their parents, brothers, sisters, friends behind, mostly never to be re-united. But parents were desperate to save their children from the horrors which they knew would come. So, by this means, some thousands of children escaped to safety and a new life. Placing that in context, 1.1 million children were to be murdered in the holocaust.

3   MEET THE FAMILY

Now, to consider my Dad and his family: our family … This picture must have been taken - I'm guessing - in the early 1920s. It is a very special picture to me - my Dad, Grandparents, Uncles, Aunts. All of them.

FRONT: In the centre are my grandparents (Henriette and Jacob).
On the left is Dad's sister Lotte and on the right is Helene (Lena).
BACK: left to right: Dad's oldest sister, Marianne, My Dad himself -
Ernst - then his oldest brother Fritz, then Walter, Gustav and Martin

Of course, I never met my paternal grandparents - Jacob died in 1931 and Henriette in 1936. Did she die from anguish and grief, as she saw something of what was happening to her eight children? She didn't see the worst.

We have noted that my Grandmother Henriette's maiden name was … Maas. She had also come from a large family. Her father's name was Gustav Maas (1826-1889). Where did that surname originally come from? Beyond the fact that it does sound Dutch rather than German, I really don't know.

I was never to meet my Uncle Fritz, nor my Aunt Marianne. But I have met all my other uncles and aunts. I was young - it was a long time ago.

So, we've met the family. What happened to these eight brothers and sisters, born into a Jewish family? All but one did get out of Germany. The following is a brief description of what happened to each of them, from my own knowledge (much of that from Reni) but also helped a lot by Franz's and Gaby's writings in which much more detail can be found. The following is intentionally a very brief account.

I'll leave my Dad (and his name) until last.

Uncle Fritz: The oldest of the brothers and sisters. Standing next to my Dad in the picture. He set up a law firm in Chemnitz in 1918 and it became successful and expanded. Life was good. Fritz and his wife Margot had 3 children - Hanna, Hilla and Franz (my cousins). This good life is well described by Franz in We Live On which is well worth my family referring to. From 1933 Fritz could not understand why the Nazis should affect him. He regarded himself as a proud German who loved his country. He had won the Iron Cross fighting in the German Army in World War I. Why should he and his family be in harm's way?

But, initially, Fritz was picked up and sent to the concentration camp at Buchenwald. After two months he returned, a broken man.

His wife Margot was unimaginably courageous. She managed to get their children away. Imagine her feelings. She arranged for Hanna (with her new daughter Tana, after much trauma at her birth due to lack of medical facilities for Jews and a subsequent horrendous journey) to Buenos Aires. Hilla came to London. Franz to Stockholm. As a boy, on well-remembered visits, I knew my cousin Hilla and her family in London quite well. She had married Rolf Sigler (another family with an horrendous story). Rolf's brother Willy and his wife Fanny (yes, that's correct) came to settle in Leicester. We knew them quite well when I was young. They were a great help to me when my Dad died.

Ultimately, with the assistance of our Uncle Martin (see below) Fritz and Margot got entry visas to Norway in the spring of 1939. There, they established themselves in the small coastal town of Asker, just west of

Oslo and settled down to build a new life. For more than three years they enjoyed being part of the community as best they could. It was just possible to arrange for their son Franz to visit from Stockholm (for two very emotional and highly valued reunions).

But shortly after Franz's last return to Sweden, the Nazis occupied Norway.

On 26th November 1942 Fritz and Margot were arrested (the spine-chilling first chapter of Franz's account relates how this happened) and began their journey to Auschwitz. Aunt Margot was murdered immediately upon arrival, on 1st December. Uncle Fritz was selected for labour but this was short-lived and on 7th January 1943, according to the archives, he too was murdered.

Their young son Franz in Stockholm (my cousin) remained unaware of his parents' fate until, shortly after the war had ended in 1945, movie theatres showed authentic images from the various concentration and extermination camps. He says, "Only then the grief swept over us".

NB: Franz tells us in We Live On: "My wife Eva has always had a very hard time sharing the story of her and her family's fate. The words to describe the hell she endured simply do not come to her. Speaking about it was, and still is, too painful for her. However, later in the book I will share an abbreviated summary of Eva's and her family's story in order to explain how our paths crossed".

So Franz has included the essentials in a separate chapter; the following are the main details. Eva lived in Hungary. She had 3 brothers and 3 sisters. The boys were drafted in 1943 into the Hungarian troops that had to do forced labour behind the German lines at the Russian front. Their fate is not recorded.

Eva's 2 older sisters, Jolan and Ersebet, 23 and 19 years old, were in Budapest but were deported to Bergen-Belsen in spring 1944. Ersebet died there.

Eva was 15 years old and she was deported to Auschwitz together with her parents, Samuel and Ethel, and her younger sister, 12 year-old Mira. Her parents and her young sister Mira were murdered immediately upon arrival.

Eva was chosen to live. After three horrendous months in the children's barrack no. 8 in Auschwitz, Eva was moved to do forced labour in a factory in Northern Germany. The German armaments industry (in her case the company Valvo, a subsidiary of Philips) needed girls with good eyes and steady hands to assemble radio valves. When the Allies began bombing the area, the factory was moved to a salt mine in the inner parts of the country.

Eva was liberated in 1945 and began her journey in a white Swedish Red Cross bus to Denmark and ultimately to Stockholm where she would eventually meet and marry my cousin Franz.

Aunt Marianne (Janne): The second oldest of the brothers and sisters. Standing on the other side of my Dad in the picture. There is much less detail about Marianne. She had not managed to emigrate but had married and become 'Marianne Rosenwald (nee Cohn)'. She divorced but was established in Berlin.

During the same period that Fritz was undertaking his 'labour' a shipment of Berlin Jews arrived at the gas chambers at Auschwitz. According to the Nazi archives, 'Marianne Rosenwald (nee Cohn)' was amongst them. Nothing more was heard of her.

Aunt Helene (Tante Lena): She married lawyer Gustav Goldstaub and lived in Rostock but came to London in 1938 and became the Aunt (with Uncle Gustav) who I recall seeing most often as a child. From time to time we travelled by steam train (marvellous!) from Leicester, then via the Central tube line to Snaresbrook Station, to their home in Hollybush Close, Wanstead. Interesting memories of wonderful things to eat, playing 'Housey Housey' (bingo in today's parlance) and lots of conversation in German which my mother and I were excluded from. These days I can understand there was much to talk about and, for my Dad, it would then have been much easier. But, perhaps surprisingly, I never learned the language (no one ever thought to teach me!).

Aunt Lotte: She was married to Norbert Kramer, the hosiery manufacturer. Their daughter is Gabriella (Gaby) and son, Helmi. After Turin and Holland, they went on eventually to settle in Denver, Colorado, USA. Gaby later settled near San Francisco and we have visited her there once. I remember Lotte as a formidable lady from when she visited once or twice when I was young.

Uncle Gustav: He became an architect and artist. He married the concert pianist Hilde Gorodetsky. They had a daughter Ruth who died of Leukaemia at a young age. They continued living in Chemnitz until they obtained visas to New Zealand in 1939 - getting out of Germany just in time. They visited Europe in the 1960s. I remember them vaguely. Gustav's painting of Mousehole, Cornwall, which he did as a gift for Dad, still hangs on our wall.

Uncle Martin: He joined his father's hosiery business in Chemnitz, becoming its star salesman. Scandinavia was its main export market. He loved hunting and fishing. He ran a commercial silver fox farm and owned a nice country house. He left Germany in 1936 to live in a posh suburb of Oslo, Norway, setting up another business importing goods from England. There was a cabin in the mountains where he hunted and fished. Martin was instrumental in helping Fritz and Margot in Norway and the reunion with their son Franz in Stockholm (for much more of this, see We Live On). At the time of Fritz and Margot's arrest Martin was warned to go into hiding. On one occasion he was assisted across the border into neutral Sweden by the Norwegian Resistance. Later, he and his second wife Josefine visited us from time to time in Leicester. I recall a larger than life Uncle Martin. They stayed at the Bell Hotel and we would sometimes meet them there - it was a fine old coaching inn. He once bought me a dart board. By the time of their next visit I had sold it and I got into real trouble!

Uncle Walter: the youngest - had a very difficult time, spending the war years in France, with Thea (who was or became his wife). I recall hearing that, as it was occupied France, they spent much of the War in hiding, eating out of dustbins and the like. They were communists. Later, Walter went on to establish a pharmaceutical manufacturing company. I vaguely recall their children, Annette and Gerard. We visited their home in Palaiseau, a suburb of Paris, when I was very young - my impression remains that I hated the trip! At some later point I remember he sent charcoal-based medicine for my mother's stomach problems.

My Dad, Ernst:
IMPORTANT: It has always been clear to me that Dad had rejected

religion - including the Jewish religion of his family. He was - and later became - a Humanist. But the following revelation which I gleaned from talking to Reni in 2008 seems very significant.

Hitler's rise in the 1930s - leading to the persecution of the Jews - led to our father deciding (at least publicly) to set aside his rejection of his family's religion, therefore making a principled stand - four-square with his family, thus opposing Hitler. Therefore, along with every other Jew in Europe he became a marked man. No doubt he would have been anyway. Even though, at the time, he probably could not foresee the full effects of the persecution, this knowledge about my father's integrity and sense of justice had a profound effect upon me when I heard about it. I like to think that I have a well-developed integrity and sense of justice and believe that, for me, these are my Dad's genes inherited in a very real sense.

But, unlike me, Dad's decision came very close to costing him his life too. When I was a teenager, I was told that Dad's name remained on the Nazi hit-list even long after the war - probably forever. Apparently Dad's opposition to Hitler extended to him becoming an active member of a 'labour' organisation. He defiantly displayed its flag at the family home until his parents told him to remove it with the words "Do you want to get us all killed?"

It is important to note that his wife Ursel and daughter Irene were not Jewish, though Reni has more recently, in passing, referred to herself as half-Jewish.

As mentioned earlier, Dad had obtained his PhD in Organic Chemistry but of course employment for Jews so qualified now became impossible. However, as related below, Dad became employed in his brother-in-law Norbert's hosiery business.

It was at about this time that Dad changed his (and Reni's) name from Cohn, adopting his mother's maiden name Maas (not a Jewish name). Franz tells us it was about 1933 but an official note added to his birth certificate since indicates it was 1935. This helped a little. I think that, in order to do that, he must have had a strong sense of the troubles to come. The following brief outline of my Dad's next 10 years or so justifies his decision. Clearly, things were going on in 1935 which were adding to the anxieties, as the following will confirm.

The Kramers' hosiery firm itself continued a little longer in Chemnitz (possibly Hitler needed socks?). At some point, Gaby's book tells us, her family escaped via Switzerland to Turin, in northern Italy, where one of 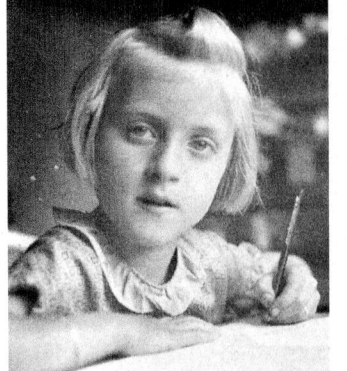 the hosiery firm's bigger customers was based. There are pictures of my Dad, in earlier, happier times, enjoying holidays in that area near Turin - so he knew where to head for when it later became so necessary.

Irene (Reni) at a young age

In 1935 Dad went on a business trip to Berlin. This is of course the beginning of the account I gave in the Introduction. His absence from home was fortunate because one evening 'they' came looking for him. Reni told me that she (age about 9) clearly recalled that she was asleep in bed and was awoken by a commotion. She remembers opening her eyes and seeing the big Gestapo boots enter her bedroom. 'They' were looking under her bed for her father. I can only speculate but I assume that, not finding him, they would re-double their efforts to despatch him on a journey to a concentration camp. **Whatever else happened, he must not return to Chemnitz.**

Somehow (maybe telephone to the firm's branch in Berlin perhaps? - we don't know but Reni says that maybe her mother went to Berlin herself), Ursel got a message to him and they agreed that they must all get out of Germany. As previously explained, this was a very difficult thing for Jews to do, even at that early stage in the persecution. The place to go for them (at that time) was Turin because family and friendly business associates were there.

As non-Jews, Ursel and Irene were able, with difficulty, to travel there. However, Gaby's description of her own somewhat traumatic experience gives a flavour of what that might have been like. By piecing together what I have been told I believe that Dad, having received the message in Berlin and so knowing that they were specifically looking for him, travelled by train from there to the Swiss border. (I've no idea whereabouts but it seems there could have been several possible routes). Wherever he was at the border he would have to cross the River Rhine or a vast lake. There was no way he could have risked a bridge or ferry. He must have had to hide somehow but under cover of darkness he found a boat and escaped across the border river or lake in this boat. As a child I remember hearing this one story about Dad's 'escape' and ever since have wondered about it and thought that this must have been part of a bigger adventure about which he should have written a book. How true!

Having arrived in Switzerland, probably as good as penniless, he walked across that country from north to south. Yes, you have read that correctly. Look at a contour map! Then he had to continue across the Italian border and on to Turin to re-join his family. That's a bold summary which no doubt masks a mass of detail - he may have got lifts for some of the way and must have needed to scrounge food somehow. Was it Summer or Winter? But Dad never spoke to me of such things. Reni has told me these essentials - she didn't know more herself; she was only about 9 years old. Why, why, oh why didn't I ask him questions when I could?

All the family in Turin became concerned about the rise of Mussolini who would eventually become Hitler's ally. Dad, Ursel and Reni with Norbert, Lotte and Gaby quickly made that move to The Hague in Holland and together established a branch of Norbert's business there.

At some point around this time Dad and Ursel parted company and divorced. It seems that Ursel had a number of crushes on other men while married to Dad; a previous one had been on a handsome fisherman while on one of their regular holidays on an island in the Baltic - I think Hiddensee. Reni tells me that the parting was not Dad's wish and he insisted on keeping Reni with him if it was to happen. Ursel had to make her choice — her new boyfriend, Epping (Eps), won the day! They married in 1936.

Holland would become occupied by the Nazis in 1940 and so, having correctly anticipated that danger ahead, Dad thought it best for him and Reni to get out of the geographical trap they were in and go across the sea to England. But the borders were closed to immigration. However, there were some exceptions, including for maids (!), nurses and for those who could provide employment. So Dad and Reni were able to move to Leicester, England. There were already friends here (Bonwitt, Sigler, Schwab, I surmise). Again for Norbert's 'global business', he and Bonwitt set up a small branch of the hosiery business in Fitzroy Street, off Hinckley Road. Dad stayed in digs at 1, Gimson Road. That name -

Gimson - would feature in later events in my life. The owners - the Barrie family - became lifelong friends. Bonwitt stayed there too and Reni recalls his prodigious appetite, causing difficulties and embarrassment due to the food shortages.

To comply with the immigration requirement, the factory employed workers to do the knitting, etc. One of the workers was Helen Widdows who lived locally in Warwick Street (my Cousin John still lives there). She was fascinated by Dad and his 'foreign' ways and his great difficulty with the language at that time. He had a habit of walking up and down the floor with his hands behind his back. She called him 'Felix' - a well-known cat food advertisement character of the time (still being used today) who apparently had this manner. Despite the fact that he spoke little English then (and never got it completely right), there was clearly an attraction, Helen being interested to some extent in current affairs, politics and so on. She was also a practising Christian, very involved with her best friend Evelyn with activities at St. Mary de Castro Church in Leicester. She and Dad married towards the end of 1939. I gather from Reni that they went on holiday to France around this time (must have been pre-war, therefore before marriage - I can only speculate). I think they must have remained living at Gimson Road for some time. A few years later they set up their own home - first at 148 Hockley Farm Road and later in Dorchester Road and at 33 Tennyson Street.

Happier times. Mum and Dad pictured at the seaside - a holiday (or honeymoon?) no doubt. Possibly in 1938 or 1939. Things were stable for a while ...

They settled down to deal with the outbreak of war as best they could. But Dad's difficulties were far from over.

4 THE WAR BEGINS

World War 2 began in September 1939. Soon, Dad was identified as an 'Enemy Alien'.

From the various accounts I have read, there was rising concern about the many 'foreigners' who had arrived on these shores - largely during many previous years but now a great many as refugees, like my Dad and Reni - escaping from the horrors of their own country, created by the Nazis.

There was increasing unease amongst politicians and the public. Within the 75,000 or so such 'foreigners', how many of them could be spies or worse? There was talk of 'The Fifth Column'. A hatred of 'aliens' grew amongst the population, no doubt whipped up through alarmist newspaper headlines. Once the unease began, and by early in 1940, it had grown to a paranoia which could not be ignored. No matter that the vast majority of those 'aliens' had in fact escaped from a tyranny in their own country or had been already settled into British life and into valuable work (like my Dad). They were almost all entirely on our side and would be valuable contributors to our war effort.

Every 'foreigner' was suddenly considered to be a potentially dangerous person - a spy or someone who would assist a German invasion. Politicians reacted with a hasty and confused policy. "Collar the lot!" - Winston Churchill's famously abrupt order was made and was applied to all 'enemy aliens' in Britain. The full story about the blunt and seemingly inhuman way in which the government at the time dealt with this perceived threat makes for sobering reading. By July 1940, 27,000 had been arrested and thousands deported to Canada, Australia, etc. It is a dark and overlooked episode in British history.

My Dad was one of those who Churchill collared. His destination was the Isle of Man - an internment camp at Onchan, just north of the main town of Douglas, one of several camps on the Island.

Imagine a lovely seaside town. In Onchan there is the curving Royal Avenue West, just set back from but facing the sea, eastwards towards

England. A row of 60 large, elegant houses were commandeered as one of the several camps on the island. The owners were turned out. The view of the sea was partially obscured by tall, secure barbed wire fences., surrounding the houses which are described in Living with the Wire:

'They were a sort of boarding house ... with about eight to ten rooms with beds in. There was a kitchen and each house - which was usually occupied by between twenty and forty people - sort of did their own cooking and collected their rations at the camp store and cooked for themselves'.

During our short visit to the Isle of Man some years ago, I bought the book Island of Barbed Wire, in which the story of the camps is told. I now have other books - Living with the Wire, which our friends Audrey (a Manx girl) and Pete bought me. More recently there is the detailed account by Simon Parkin, The Island of Extraordinary Captives, only just published in 2022. In itself, it is an amazing story of the background and of life in captivity, both terrible and extraordinary. There is of course more on the web and I have 2 or 3 of the special Onchan coins which were the currency there.

The internees set up a substantial social life, producing an internal newspaper called the Onchan Pioneer of which 47 editions were published. There was a major lecture scheme which became known as 'The Popular University'. I note there was a course in chemistry and have to wonder if Dad was perhaps involved with that. There were fitness regimes, debating societies, etc. so the time probably wasn't too unpleasant, if the conditions and the captivity itself could be ignored. For a few, the working day involved agriculture where no doubt Dad learned some of his vegetable-growing skills. I found a passage of great interest in The Island of Extraordinary Captives, which focusses on a different camp (Hutchinson) but I assume there must have been similarities:

There were opportunities, too, for those who wanted to work outside the camp. From September 1940, the younger camp members were permitted to take on local farm work. After rollcall, volunteers would meet by Hutchinson's gate and wait for news as to whether one of the local farmers required help that day. If they were fortunate, the young men would be collected and - under armed guard - set to work picking and sorting potatoes, pulling out carrots, mangolds and turnips, threshing or spreading manure. The feeling of leaving the camp was 'something like liberty', as one volunteer put it. 'Standing on the field, looking at the hills, plains and forests around you, amidst all the beauty of the nature with a wide sky above you and the free soil beneath your feet, doing a useful job and so connected with the free people, you forget your sorrows and feel yourself free.' These excursions brought contact with the islanders, whose sympathetic reaction revitalised the mental health of men who had lived under the cloud of suspicion for the past few months.

Reading this one passage has given me a new and special insight into my Dad's story. I well remember his love for the countryside, open spaces, for organic gardening, his very large allotment and the endless sacks of potatoes and fertiliser in the shed at home. I am as certain as I can be that he acquired a dream of becoming a small farmer. There were a number of books on the subject on the bookshelves at home. He joined the Soil Association but no doubt his dream was impossible and therefore unrealised.

Thankfully, Dad had not been one of those selected for internment in Canada. Apparently Paul Schneller (eventually to become Reni's husband and my brother-in-law) was interned on the island too, before being transferred to an internment camp in Canada. By chance, he was not transferred on the *SS Anandora Star* which a U-boat sank off Ireland with the loss of 805 internees' lives.

I can only imagine Helen's thoughts. Barely married and her husband whisked away with no indication how long for. She suffered too. I'm certain there was a lot of support for her from friends and family during the time Ernst was in captivity. I think she remained living at Gimson Road. After an appeal, assisted by a good friend, Eric Hancock, Dad was released from internment on 16th June 1941. Eric had come to the rescue. Using his British Council influence he persuaded the powers-that-be that Dad would be far more useful to the war effort running a market garden here and was no threat to national security. And so it happened! Dad came home earlier than might have been the case and was set up with a market garden at Groby (or was it Groby Road? - more likely I think). He filled a wheelbarrow with the vegetables he had grown, pushing it around Leicester streets, selling them to housewives. But this was not a financial success and he failed to earn a sufficient living. I can only imagine that this masked many difficulties. Friends and family must have helped out quite a lot.

Reni has since told me: "Dad was stationed near Douglas and worked for a very nice farmer (hard work though). But he had affectionate feelings towards the town, of which you are living proof".

So that probably answers the second question: why my name is Douglas!

5   RECOVERY

From around this time, Reni has told me, upon return home Dad became very depressed and difficult to live with. Not surprising. He was living through the multiple heartbreaks of losing so much: his Country and all he had known there, his brother, sister and sister-in-law to Hitler's gas chambers, the others all scattered, mostly beyond reach, around the world. The knowledge of all of that would have gradually become apparent to him, bit by bit. He would not have been able to see his mother, Henriette before she died in 1936 (his father, Jacob had died in 1931). I know little of my paternal grandparents other than from Gaby's book.

Dad had lost any opportunity to excel as a scientist. He had lost his first wife. He had lost his freedom while interned.

He had to grapple with the need to adopt a new country and language. There was still his beloved daughter Irene - though she would soon be living and working away from home, in London. She ultimately emigrated to the USA in 1959.

He could so easily have lost his life. I would not be here to tell this story.

But I like to think there was also happiness. A new wife, Helen (married 1939) - and my eventual arrival in 1944 when he was 46 (Mum 44). Perhaps we offered him a new beginning and a slow recovery. I cannot remember Dad as anything other than a Great Dad, albeit quite an older, 'different' and tired one! Dad and Reni became naturalised UK citizens in April 1947.

At this point I suppose I should insert a note of my own arrival on the scene. If internment hadn't intervened I might now be two or three years older, I suppose.

Eventually, I was born on 17th May 1944 - Douglas Edward Maas. (Why Douglas? Reni must be right - Dad must have had some affection for that place in the Isle of Man). Our address then was 148 Hockley Farm Road, Leicester although I was born at a maternity home at 56

Clarendon Park Road, Leicester, a large elegant building but now a block of offices.

I was my Mother's first and only child. She was 44 and had a very rough time of my birth. My crying went on forever, I've been told. Difficult for all of us, I guess. Dad was 46. But there must have been something of a buzz in the air during my very earliest days, as 20 days later the D-Day Landings - Operation Overlord - would take place. Mount Vesuvius erupted that year too! And Health Minister Mr. Henry Willink set out the Conservative Government's proposals for a National Health Service (to be initiated by Labour in 1948).

When I arrived, we were living through the tremendous austerity and hardships of the Second World War. These hardships were to continue for a further 11 years following the end of the War in 1945, as rationing continued on, finally coming to an end in 1956. We lived on minimal rations, National dried milk and National orange juice for children, an ounce of butter, one egg at a time. All basic stuff - no pineapples, bananas or anything else imported for a long time. We saved every bit of paper, string and so on. Newspaper was used in the toilet; it would eventually become my task to tear it into squares ready for use, making holes near the corner so bundles could be hung on a hook with string. That continued into the 1950s.

At some time after my birth, there was a brief move to Dorchester Road but then we moved to 33 Tennyson Street, Leicester in the area of Leicester known as Highfields.

A great Dad

This is the first house I can remember. It was a fairly upmarket tall narrow old terraced house with a useful large attic room (from where I once fell down the attic stairs). The front doorstep was red and it seemed to need polishing with Cardinal Red polish at very frequent intervals. The hallway was dark and very Victorian with coloured floor tiles, stairs going up and doors

30

leading off. There was a small, dark yard at the back with high brick walls and where a few plants sought out a bit of light to grow. That's where the coal shed and outside toilet was, heated with a paraffin lamp in Winter - not for warmth but to prevent the pipes freezing. I'll never forget the smell of a paraffin lamp.

A back gate led into an entry serving several of the adjacent terraced houses and which in turn led to Beckingham Road, the main road just around the corner. The entry always seemed to be full of dog poo, to be avoided.

I only ever knew one grandparent, Mum's mother Jane, who stayed with us there until a ripe old age. She lived in the front downstairs room, complete with bed and commode. Apparently I spent a lot of time with her. I don't recall much of that but it has occurred to me that 4 or 5 year old boys might tend to take a slightly unhealthy interest in commodes and the use being made of them. She had died by the time I was about 5. Of course I never met another grandparent but cousin John reminds me that our Grandfather was Edward (maybe significant) and that he had been a builder's labourer.

From the few years we lived at Tennyson Street, until I was 6, I remember quite a lot. But of course events are a bit of a jumble, not necessarily in neat chronological order! For example the living or back room was where we must have existed most of the time. Always rather dark with dim light bulbs. I recall the table, my toys on the floor, the open fire and the battles with draught excluders. Upstairs there must have been 3 bedrooms. I remember clearly where those attic stairs went up from the landing; I fell down them once. I have no recollection at all of a bathroom. There should have been one because Highfields was in a better part of town. For some reason, washing and cleaning my teeth (in the kitchen) remains strong in my memory - dipping my toothbrush into pink powder contained in a small flat round tin. I also remember well that National dried milk in purple tins and the orange juice essential for children's health. Bars of soap were used up as far as possible and the small remaining pieces collected with others in a small wire cage with a handle. This was then swished vigorously in the washing-up water to be used for dish washing.

All this was at the height of post-war rationing which didn't completely end until 1956. It seemed to produce healthy kids. I am sure my Dad's pre-occupation with growing vegetables organically had something to do with it. There's a very vague memory of going to Dad's market garden which he either kept on, maybe part time, or maybe it was a garden allotment nearer home. Allotments would feature strongly in the coming years.

It took a long time to re-build the country but things very slowly changed. Milk and coal deliveries by horse and cart changed to milk float and lorries. Fetching coke from the gas works for the open fires at home. No phone, TV, fridge, washing machine, supermarkets and all of that until much later. Commodities such as sugar, butter and biscuits sold loose and weighed and packed by the assistant behind the counter at the grocers. Steam trains until the late 1960s.

A simpler existence. I lived through all that and I was very happy.

In this story there is something missing. I simply do not know what happened to the knitwear factory after Dad was whisked off to the Isle of Man. Probably Bonwitt was interned as well - he later appears in Dad's address book living in London. Was it just abandoned, sold, bombed? Even though close to the city centre, it is now a leafy, almost rural in appearance, residential area with no remaining evidence of any factory. Dad certainly did not return to it, as the following pages will indicate. That is a mystery.

Ultimately, an acquaintance - Oplatek - who had set up the English Glass Company, gave Dad a job. My birth certificate states that Dad's job title was 'glass presser'. He was there for a few years because I clearly remember that for some reason I was taken to see him at work. I have an indelible memory of him sitting at a furnace wearing a sweat band around his head, making glass buttons (or cats eye lenses). That 'Dante's inferno' vision is my most vivid (and probably earliest) childhood memory. Oh, my poor Dad - he was an intellectual, a scientist - Dr. E.H. Maas, PhD - not a manual worker.

Some written records show that the company had seven furnaces. So Dad was the operator at one of those. The factory was in Empire Road, off Tudor Road, not far from where we lived prior to Tennyson Street. English Glass is now listed as a dormant company. More recently I have obtained a slim booklet about English Glass. It's written by one of the Directors and indicates that the company was originally set up as an offshoot of the John Bull Rubber Company. The company was making

Cat's Eyes - the famous 1933 road safety invention by Percy Shaw who had been a road mender in Halifax. It seems that a separate company was needed to make the glass lenses to install into the rubber bases. This varies a bit from the official history of cat's eyes but maybe John Bull was just a sub-contractor. So, I am guessing that after some discussion Dad managed to get a transfer to John Bull where he became the Technical Librarian (see below). That was undoubtedly a valuable and welcome promotion, giving him an important move, much closer to his background and skills. And indeed much closer to where we lived.

Money was almost certainly tight. Dad tried to be an entrepreneur. As a chemist, he invented a cleaning product which he called EMAAZIN (I remember little phials of liquid mounted on cards bearing this name). He also sold nylon stockings. They were an important commodity in those days and came in flat white boxes and were in different colours and sizes. His interest in stamp collecting led him to become something of a mail order stamp dealer and was always sending out envelopes with the little blue approval books and doing endless records and accounts. I guess I eventually turned out much the same - a budding entrepreneur with similar lack of success! Neither of us were destined to be salesmen - it's either in the genes or it's not! In later life I would regret not appreciating this much earlier.

I feel I should mention one distinct memory I have from around that time. Dad was clearly connected with many friends and acquaintances in Leicester - those with similar experiences or involved in some way. I recall very clearly that we made several visits - for tea I think - to a house not far away, near Victoria Park. This was the Attenborough family home and we had tea with Mary Attenborough, the mother of Richard and David who, I surmise, were away at university (maybe my sister knew them - a similar age). Interestingly I recall there was a large world globe on display in the front room and also some Russian dolls which I was allowed to play with as I found them fascinating. I have only recently made the important connection - that Mary Attenborough was instrumental in organising some of the Kindertransport (referred to earlier) and indeed the family went on to adopt two girls from Berlin who became Richard and David's 'adopted sisters'. Local man, Richard Graves, has recently published The Life and Times of Mary Attenborough (1896-1961) (see references) telling her remarkable story.

When I was about six years old, we moved house to Wicklow Drive and, I am sure that the time there - just a few years - was probably our happiest as a family. It was close to Dad's large allotment and we had a lovely garden at home. Some happy memories there.

Because Mum was becoming increasingly unwell, we moved again when I was a teenager to Staveley Road. She died in 1964 when I was 20. I was so sad of course but it was yet another tremendous loss for Dad.

A happy moment but Mum was becoming increasingly   unwell   ...

Eventually Dad's employer, John Bull, was taken over by Dunlop and before long Dad was made redundant. This was not too long before his retirement and so for just a few years he became employed by Gimson & Company in Vulcan Road. For a short time after I passed my driving test and when Dad had bought me a 1938 Morris 10 for £35, I used to pick him up from work. There is that name again - Gimson. It would figure significantly later in my life.

I was probably about 23 when Dad was about 69 and he decided that the Staveley Road house would become too much for him on his own, as I was to marry within a year in 1967. He searched for an alternative place to live.

A   proud   Dad   at   my   wedding

It has always been my regret that I - being young and with so many other things on my mind - could not offer him more help. I think his idea was to move to somewhere close to our first home which was to be at Birstall, a village just north of Leicester. He actually ended up on the very top floor of one of the tower blocks at Goodwood. Merton House has thankfully since been demolished. The 23rd floor may have offered tremendous views but was as far away from his beloved garden as it could possibly be.

In June 1968 Marilyn and I were enjoying our holiday. Marilyn was pregnant with our first child who would be born in October. We were cruising our small hired motor cruiser past Acle on the River Bure on the Norfolk Broads, heading for Great Yarmouth and the southern rivers. As we passed the Acle boatyard, we noticed one of those large black notice boards which were then used to convey important messages to passing boats, long before there were mobile phones.

The message gave the name of our boat and the instruction to urgently telephone the police in Leicester. Thus we discovered that Dad had unexpectedly died of a heart attack (a broken heart?) in his flat on the top floor of Merton House. He had been discovered by the caretaker.

So, the ultimate sadness - my Dad had died alone, aged 70. The thought still often haunts me. I just wish I had known him for much longer and that I had been a better and more understanding son. I had left him alone when I married.

I really wish I had asked him so many more questions.

6 BEYOND

That was the story of why our family name is Maas. If my Dad hadn't made those momentous decisions, including changing his name, myself and my family probably would not exist.

So, who am I?

Everyone's life is full of interest. How could it be otherwise? In my case it has not been quite so dramatic but it has been a bumpy ride. I had a good start, didn't I? I am the son of a refugee immigrant. My genes are a mixture from Saxony and from England and so, perhaps flippantly, I can claim to be a genuine Anglo-Saxon. That is as may be but I grew up very much as an Englishman and proud to be so. I doubt that anyone has ever been able to detect anything else in me. That's just how it is.

From the beginning I only ever sought a quiet, peaceful, uneventful life but somehow a lot of extraordinary events just kept happening. I am not clever in the academic sense. My father and my son both have PhDs and so, I quip, my brains skipped a generation. However I am the product of the University of Life with numerous experiences which others might find interesting.

The question is - does someone have to be a high profile, highly paid celebrity in the public eye to have had an interesting life? Do they need to be in the world of entertainment, sport, industry, business, politics or what have you? Perhaps an explorer, a ground-breaking scientist or infamous dictator?

The answer is NO! Rich or poor, famous or obscure, clever or not - just about everyone has a fascinating tale to tell … always worth the effort to write it down and well worth a reader becoming absorbed in the story. Picking up on this thought, as an ordinary guy with a whole variety of twists and turns on my roller-coaster ride of a lifetime, I decided that the whole story - my Autobiography - might be of interest to others. There are sure to be some useful lessons.

Of course, this - my Dad's story, is the basis of the first chapter. An essential introduction to my own autobiography. I have written my warts-and-all tale set against the background of many of the events of the last 75 years. My life may not have been quite so dramatic, or sad. However, it has been something of a page-turner!

Would you find it interesting? So far, my family has seen it. Should I publish it? It now has up to date revisions. Letting the wider world see it might be the next step. Should I or shouldn't I? Look out for

The (Un)eventful Life of Douglas E. Maas
(75 years from WW-2 to Covid-19)

AFTERTHOUGHT

I find coincidences quite interesting. You might find these of interest:

In Franz's account, We Live On, he writes of his mother:

Margot was born on August 2nd, 1892 as the long-awaited daughter of Elise and Salo (Salomon) Bermann in the German town of Gleiwitz in Upper Silesia (Oberschlesien). Today it is called Gliwice and is in Poland. Salo was a physician and his patients were both German townsfolk in Gleiwitz and Polish farmers from the surrounding countryside. In his memoirs, their son Gottfried wrote that his father was often collected in the middle of the night in a farmer's horse-drawn cart to go to a difficult childbirth. These Polish farmers often paid in kind rather than with currency, meaning the Bermann family household rarely lacked for eggs or poultry. Gottfried also describes a folk remedy that farmers used to heal particularly nasty wounds; spreading mouldy cheese on the wound! This was many decades before Alexander Fleming's Nobel discovery of penicillin.

(NB: Sir Alexander Fleming's Nobel Prize-winning discovery was made in 1928 - many years after the events described above!)

As I mentioned, I visited the Holocaust Centre (some 50 miles by road from home) where I joined in with a large group of Year 5 school pupils to listen to survivor Hedi Argent tell her story of the Kindertransport. It just so happens that those pupils were visiting from Braunstone Frith Junior School in Leicester. That's less than half a mile (almost within sight) of my first ever address in 1944, at 148, Hockley Farm Road, Leicester. I find that a curious coincidence, somehow completing a circle.

"Living well is the best revenge"

SOME REFERENCES

The National Holocaust Centre and Museum: Acre Edge Road, Laxton, Newark, Nottinghamshire NG22 0PA

The Good Place, Gabriella Mautner. 2006 Replica Books. ISBN: 0-735-10598-7 (she has also written other books on the subject)

We Live On, A Family Chronicle, Notes by Franz Cohn

Two Brothers, a novel by Ben Elton. 2012 Black Swan.   ISBN 978-0-552-77531-1

The Life and Times of Mary Attenborough (1896-1961) by Richard Graves. Foreword by David Attenborough. 2022 The Book Guild Ltd. ISBN 978-1914471148

Island of Barbed Wire, Connery Chappell. 1984 Corgi Books. ISBN 0-552-12712-4

Living with the Wire, Edited by Yvonne M Cresswell for Manx National Heritage 1994, revised 2010. ISBN 978-0-901106-63-6

The Island of Extraordinary Captives, Simon Parkin. 2022 Sceptre Books. ISBN 978-1-529-34722-7

Collar the Lot! by Peter and Leni Gillman. 1980 Quartet Books. ISBN 978-0704334083

Collar the Lot! A one hour BBC 'Archive on Four' programme

Archive, compiled by me, available to the family in due course ...

Of course there's a mass of information available about the key events   described

39

ABOUT THE AUTHOR

I have spent a long lifetime discovering information about my Dad's remarkable story.

The dramatic escape by rowing boat was just a small part of it all. Endurance, tragedy, horror, escape, then captivity, sadness but ultimate happiness ...

Eventually, I realised that all of this was a story worth telling ...

My own story ... ? Well, it is that of a late developer who did not achieve a lot at Grammar school but went on to become something of a roller-coaster ride at the University of Life. Let's say it's been interesting.

I've been writing and publishing all kinds of things, mostly factual books and periodicals for interest groups, for more than 60 years. A recent departure is a novel (they say everyone has a novel in them) called *Dead Wood*. It's a murder mystery and available on Amazon kindle/unlimited/paperback.

Printed in Great Britain
by Amazon

80642891R00031